For Oskar and Jazmin who've walked with Handstand for over half their lives. – GMN

© Text Gina M Newton 2020
© Illustrations Rachel Tribout 2020

All rights reserved. Except under the conditions described in the *Australian Copyright Act 1968* and subsequent amendments, no part of this publication may be reproduced, stored in a retrieval system or transmitted in any form or by any means, electronic, mechanical, photocopying, recording, duplicating or otherwise, without the prior permission of the copyright owner. Contact CSIRO Publishing for all permission requests.

The author and illustrator assert their moral rights, including the right to be identified as a creator.

A catalogue record for this book is available from the National Library of Australia.

ISBN: 9781486311842 (hbk)
ISBN: 9781486311859 (epdf)

Published by:

CSIRO Publishing
Locked Bag 10
Clayton South VIC 3169
Australia

Telephone: +61 3 9545 8400
Email: publishing.sales@csiro.au
Website: www.publish.csiro.au

Edited by Sally McInnes
Cover, internal design and layout by Rachel Tribout
Printed in China by Leo Paper Products Ltd.

The views expressed in this publication are those of the author and illustrator and do not necessarily represent those of, and should not be attributed to, the publisher or CSIRO.

Note for readers: Scientific terms are explained in the glossary at the end of the book.

Note for teachers: Teacher notes are available at:
https://www.publish.csiro.au/book/7903#forteachers

HOLD ON!
SAVING THE SPOTTED HANDFISH

Written by
Gina M Newton

Illustrated by
Rachel Tribout

MY NAME'S HANDSTAND, AND I'M A SPOTTED HANDFISH.

That's when dinosaurs roamed Earth and its oceans.

I'm one of the few fish species alive **TODAY** that a dinosaur could have recognised.

Like all anglerfish, I have a fleshy **GROWTH** sticking out from my head.

It acts like a fishing **ROD** and **LURE**.

I use my lure to catch food. I like to eat little worms and crustaceans from the sandy seafloor.

In deep-sea species, this lure can **LIGHT UP**.

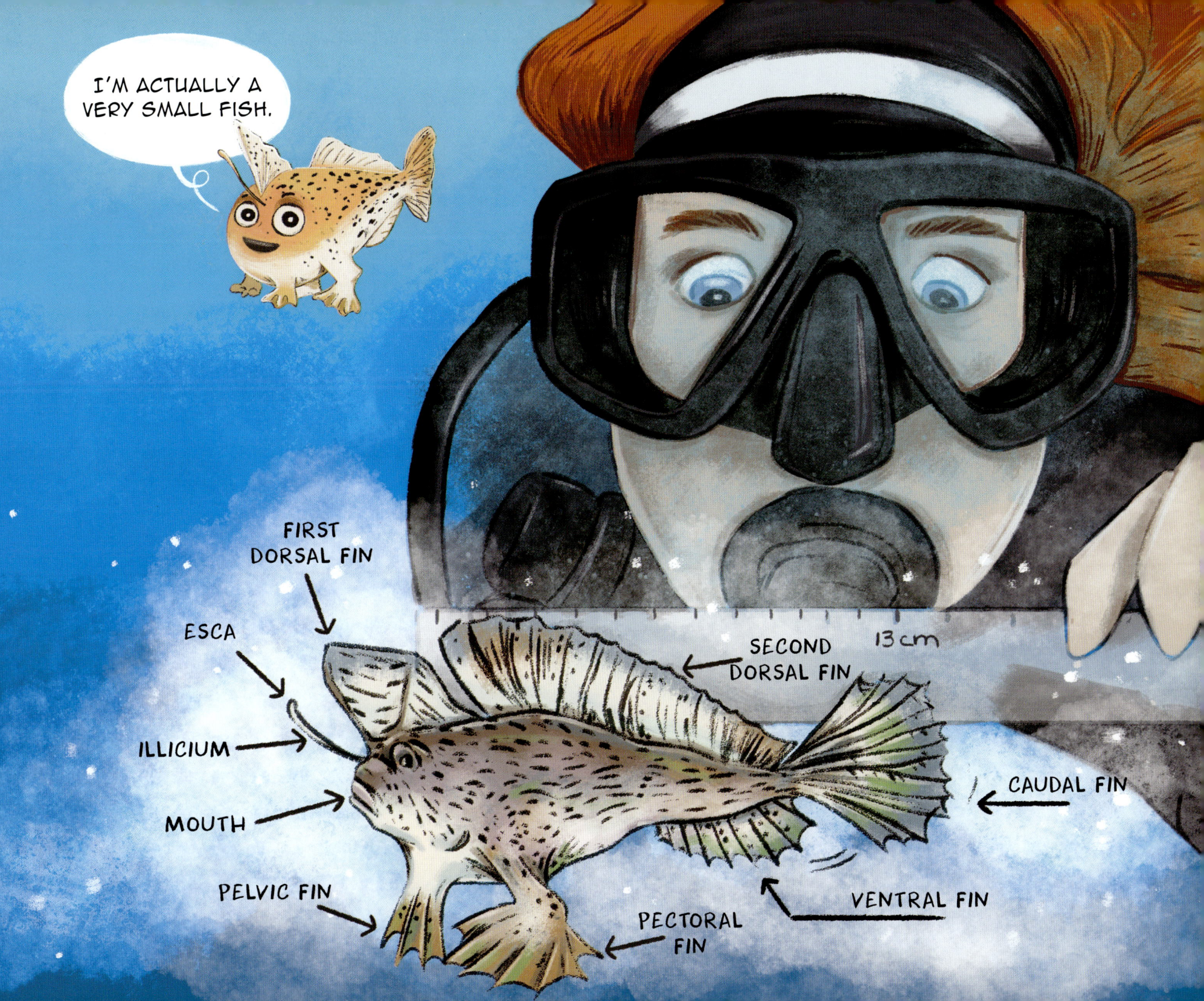

NEWSFLASH! I AM VERY FAMOUS FOR TWO IMPORTANT REASONS.

REASON WHY I'M FAMOUS: **NUMBER 1**

I HAVE HANDS!

Well, they're really pectoral fins that look a bit like human hands.

They come in very handy too.

I live right on the seafloor, so to move about I just walk on my hands.

It's pretty **SLOW GOING** though.

Most fish swim – BUT I DON'T.

That's because handfish haven't got a swim bladder.

A swim bladder helps a fish to rise above the seafloor, and to move up and down through the water.

It controls buoyancy.

But, if I get scared,
I can use my powerful tail
to quickly DART away for a short distance.

But most other fish species hatch from their eggs as larvae.

Fish larvae become part of the plankton and are carried away by ocean currents to settle in **FAR-OFF** places.

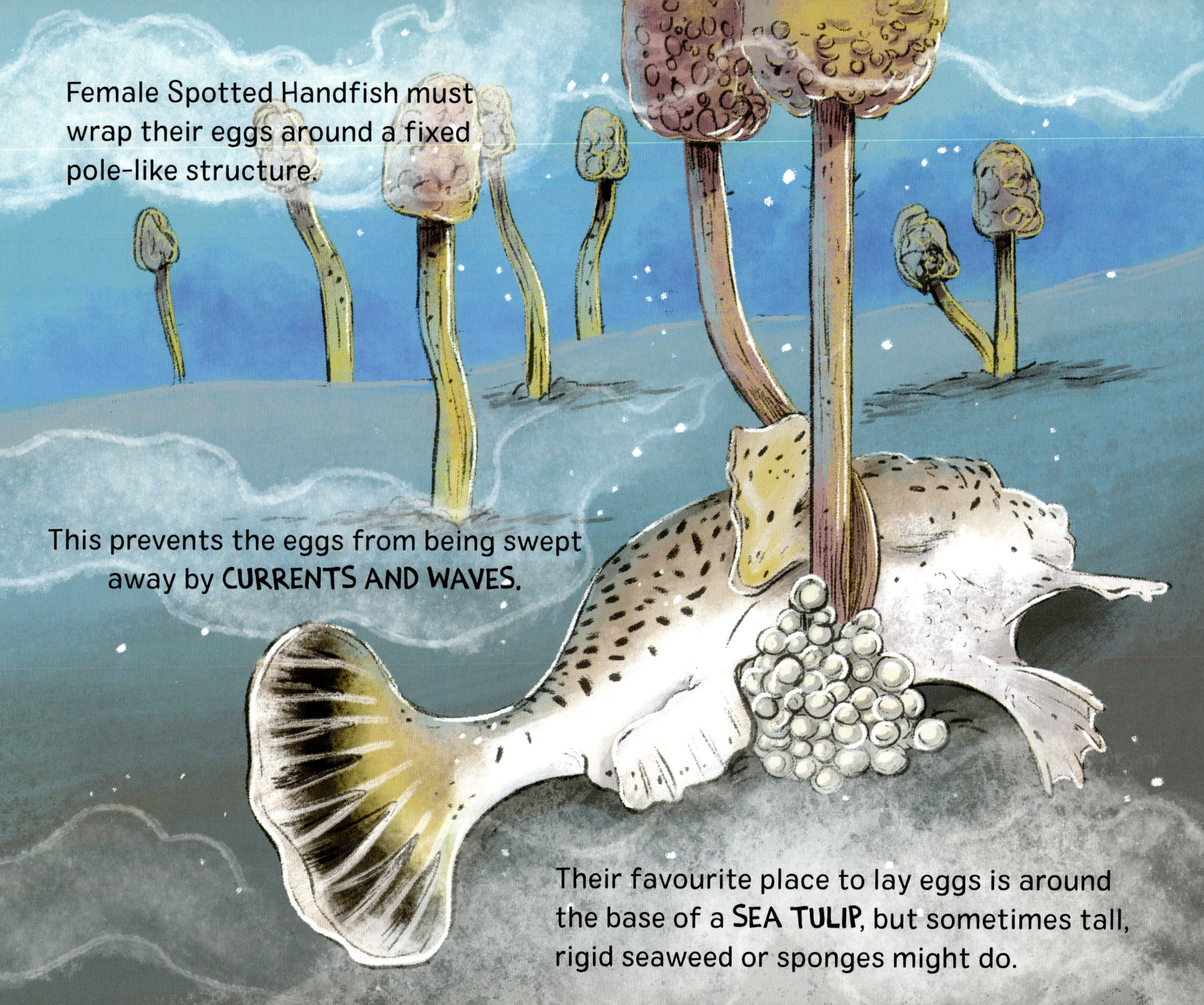

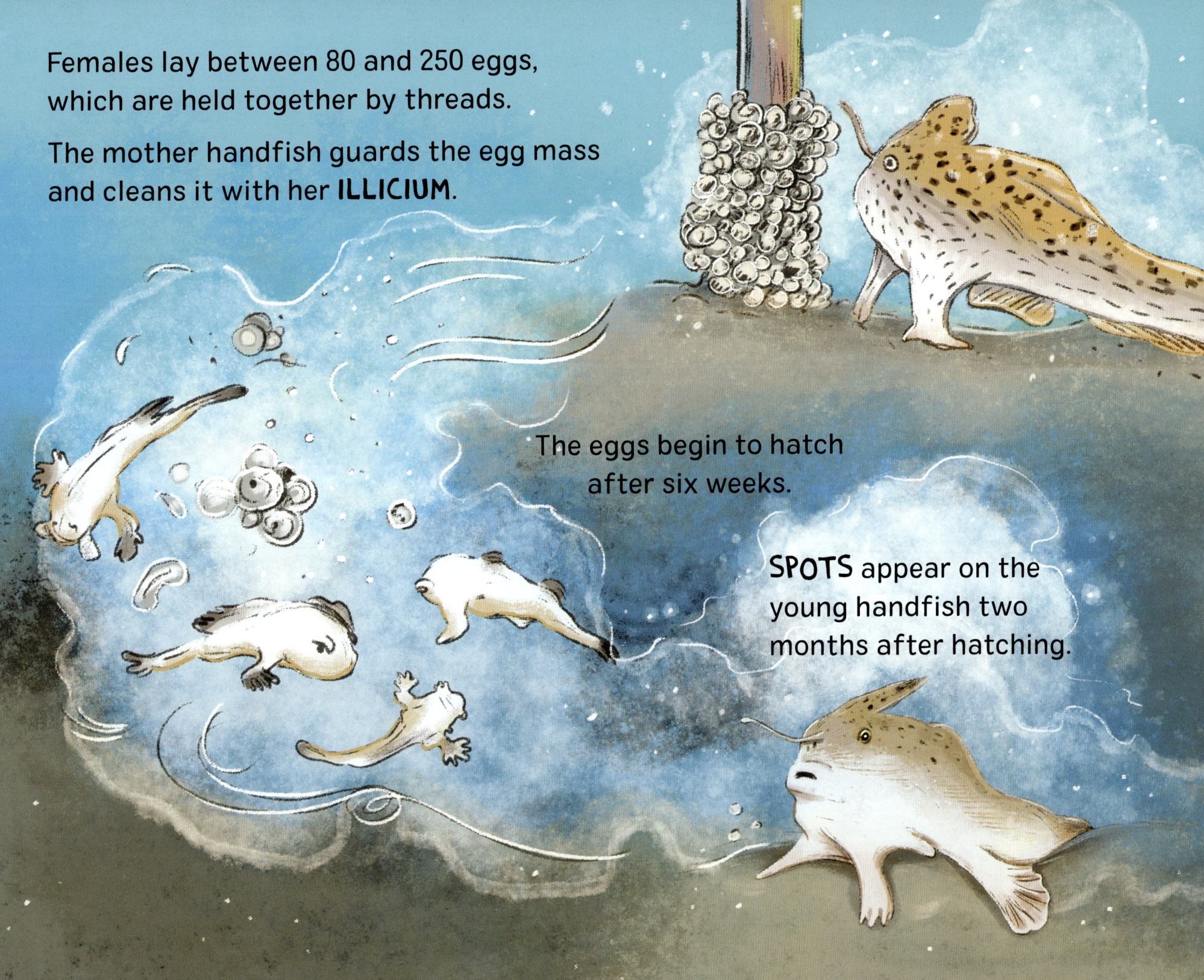

A few decades ago, the number of Spotted Handfish became so small that my species was close to disappearing **FOREVER**.

REASON WHY I'M FAMOUS: NUMBER 2. TA DA!

We were heading for **EXTINCTION**!

BREAKING NEWS
$1.20
21 September 1982
Spotted Handfish: NEXT ON THE LINE?

IUCN: International Union for the Conservation of Nature

Luckily, the scientists noticed, and the Spotted Handfish was included on the world's special **RED LIST** of Threatened Species.

We were one of the first marine fish species on that list, but now there are **EVEN MORE!**

THREATENED SPECIES RED LIST

VAQUITA PORPOISE
CORROBOREE FROG
BLACK RHINO
GILBERT'S POTOROO
ORANGE BELLIED PARROT
SUMATRAN TIGER
EASTERN GORILLA
ZIEBELL'S HANDFISH
SPOTTED HANDFISH
RED HANDFISH
GREY NURSE

Around 100 to 50 million years ago, there were hundreds of different handfish species living in the world's oceans.

But nearly all of these became **EXTINCT** a long time ago due to natural changes in Earth's history.

Today, there are only 14 species left, or maybe less. And guess what? **THEY ARE ALL AUSSIES!**

They all inhabit the coastal marine waters of south-eastern Australia.

The conditions in this region allowed these handfish species to survive – up until now.

These days, you can only find my species in a small area near Hobart, **TASMANIA**.

Spotted Handfish, like a few of my relatives, are in **SERIOUS TROUBLE**.

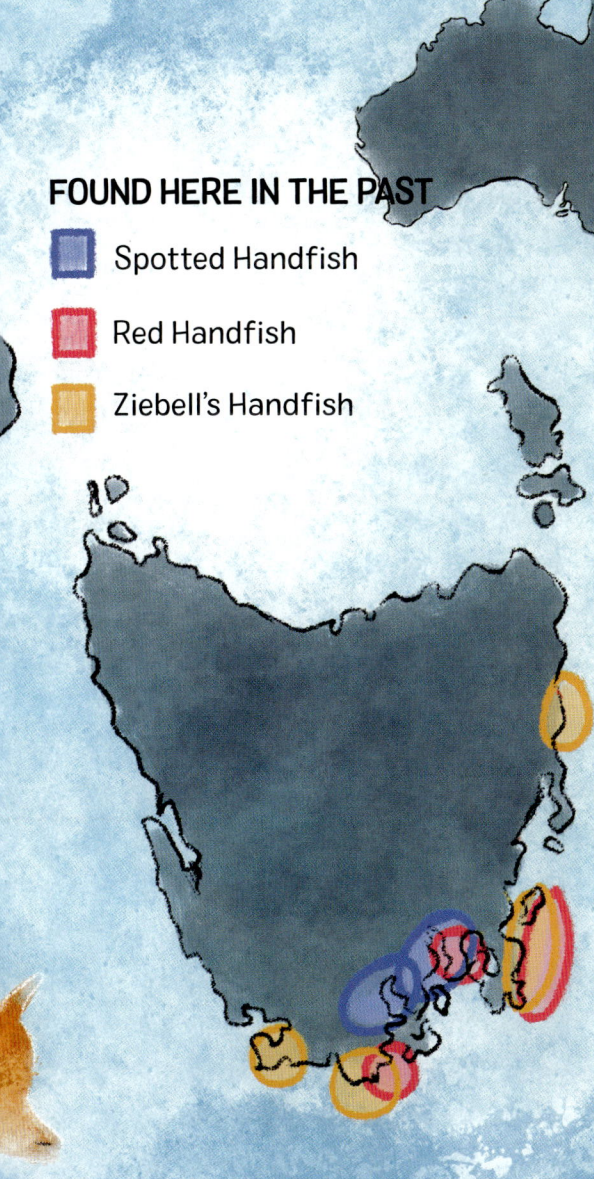

FOUND HERE IN THE PAST
- Spotted Handfish
- Red Handfish
- Ziebell's Handfish

Lucky I'm on that **RED LIST**, or I could end up the same way as the Tasmanian Tiger – **EXTINCT!**

Some of my relatives are in trouble too.

Here's the latest CONSERVATION UPDATE.

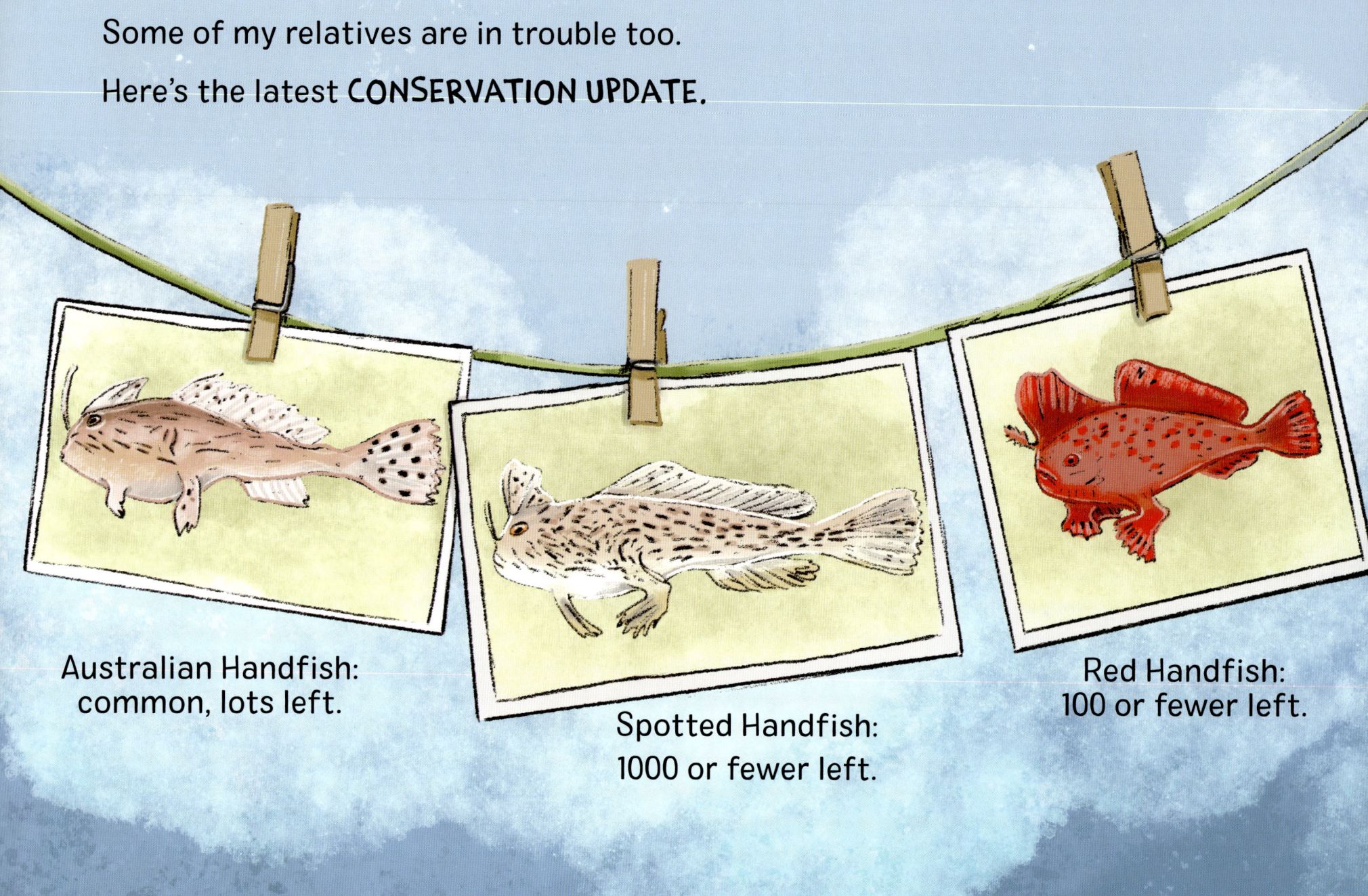

Australian Handfish: common, lots left.

Spotted Handfish: 1000 or fewer left.

Red Handfish: 100 or fewer left.

Ziebell's Handfish: not seen for 15 years.

Pink Handfish: not seen for 20 years.

Smooth Handfish: only known from old scientific records.

Eight other handfish species live in areas where the water is much deeper. But not much is known about them, apart from a few museum specimens collected a very long time ago.

I'M SORRY TO SAY THAT THOSE RELATIVES NOT SEEN FOR A VERY LONG TIME COULD ALREADY BE EXTINCT!

SO WHY AM I IN TROUBLE?

If there are threats or if my habitat changes, there is not much I can do.

Check out why ...

VULNERABILITY CHECKLIST

- ☑ I can't swim
- ☑ I live in a small area
- ☑ I don't have planktonic larvae
- ☑ I can't move fast or far away
- ☑ I need a special structure for laying eggs
- ☑ I live mostly in shallow waters
- ☑ I am very small

And there are many **THREATS** that a Spotted Handfish must face.

higher water temperatures from climate change

fishing nets and dredges

being eaten by predators

pollution from chemicals

smothering from soil washed in from the land

rubbish

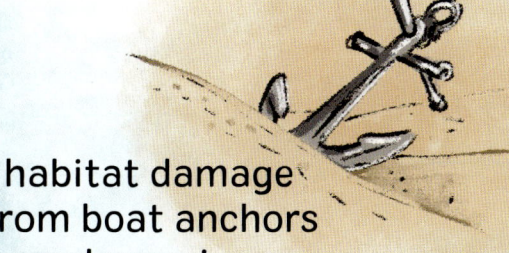
habitat damage from boat anchors and moorings

illegal capture for aquariums

competition for space and food

The seastars multiplied in the millions.

The invaders ate everything in their path, including most of the Sea Tulips.

Nothing was left for the Spotted Handfish to lay their eggs around.

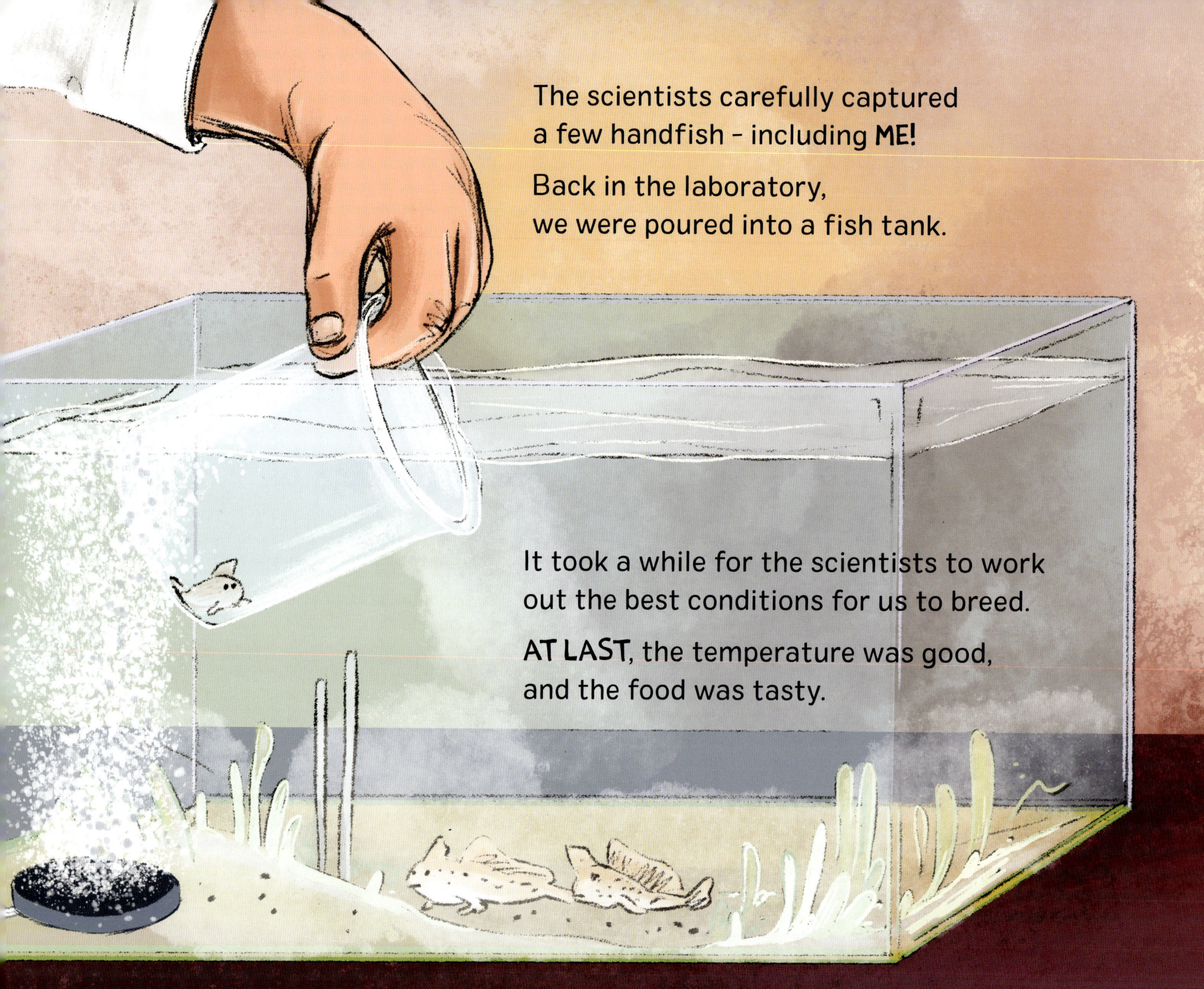

The scientists also gave us plastic poles to wrap our eggs around.

And it worked – EGGS WERE SOON LAID!

The male handfish fertilised the eggs while flashing their fins in a fancy mating dance.

After our captive breeding success, the scientists put most of us back in the sea.

An artist had made tough **CERAMIC POLES** that looked and felt like Sea Tulip stems. Ceramic was better for the sea. It didn't break apart like plastic poles could.

The scientists had placed **HUNDREDS** of ceramic poles around the seafloor of my habitat.

The female Spotted Handfish loved laying their eggs around these poles.

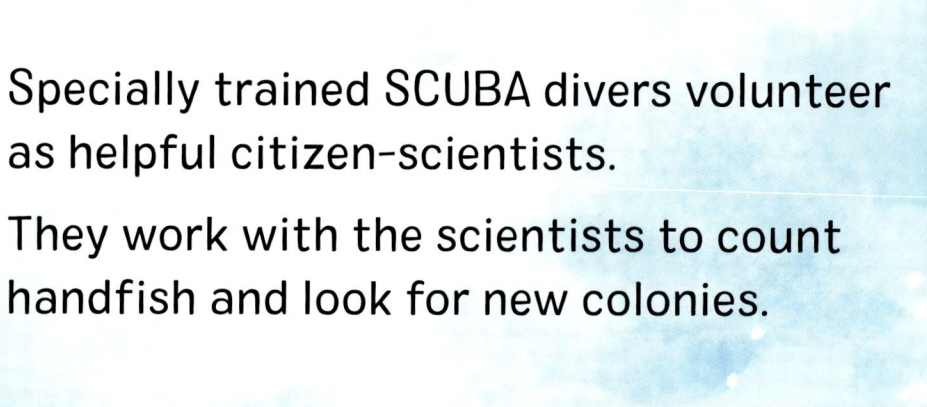

Specially trained SCUBA divers volunteer as helpful citizen-scientists.

They work with the scientists to count handfish and look for new colonies.

The divers really like it when I do a **HANDSTAND.**

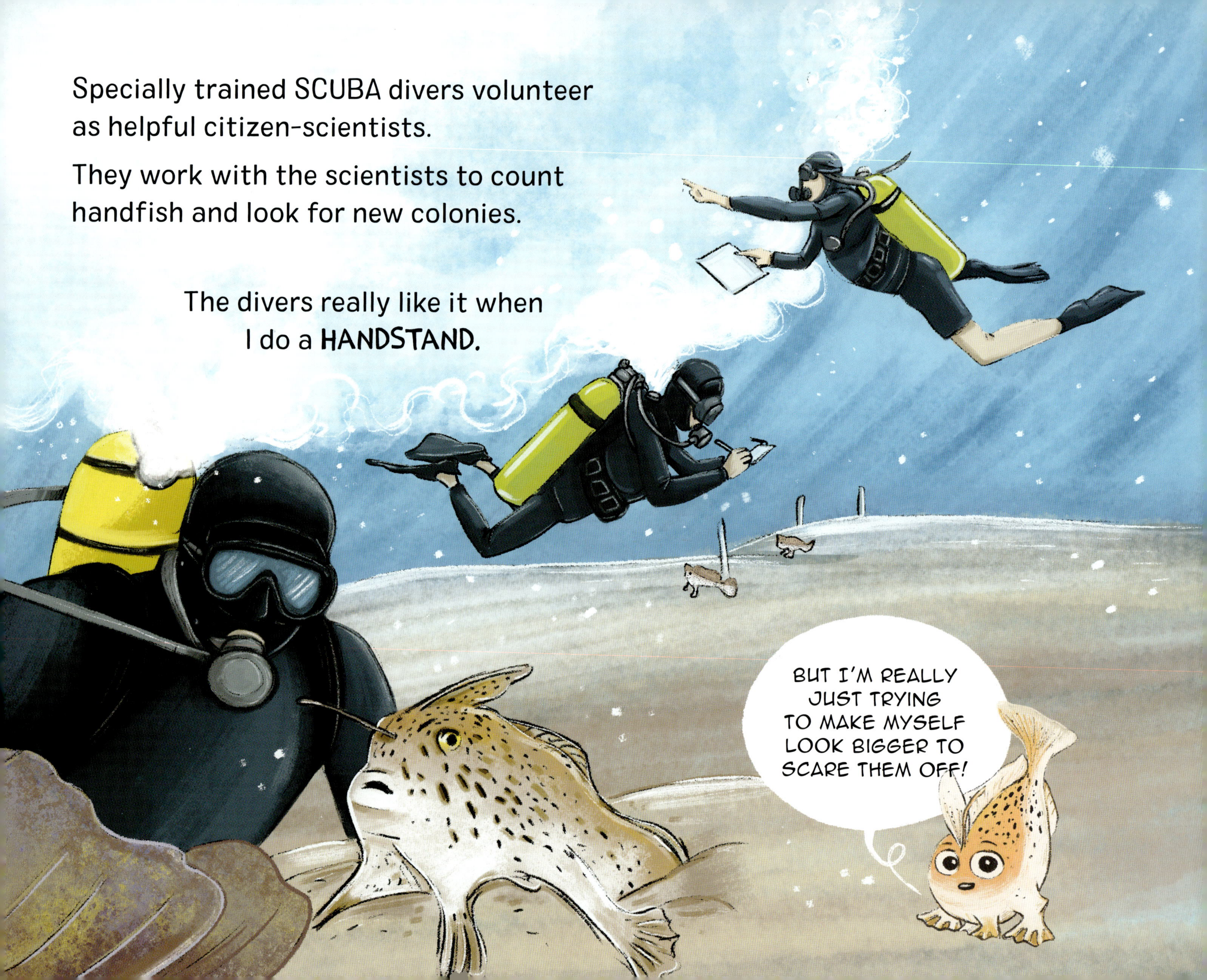

BUT I'M REALLY JUST TRYING TO MAKE MYSELF LOOK BIGGER TO SCARE THEM OFF!

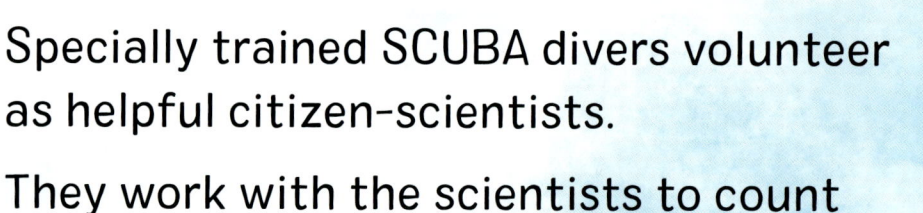

Specially trained SCUBA divers volunteer as helpful citizen-scientists.

They work with the scientists to count handfish and look for new colonies.

The divers really like it when I do a **HANDSTAND.**

BUT I'M REALLY JUST TRYING TO MAKE MYSELF LOOK BIGGER TO SCARE THEM OFF!

GLOSSARY AND ABBREVIATIONS

Alien: Belonging to another country or place; non-native.

Anglerfish: A fish that lures prey with a fleshy lobe sticking out from its large head; its body is often small.

Aquarium: A glass tank used for housing fish and aquatic plants.

Ballast water: Water carried in a ship's ballast tanks to improve balance and stability while at sea; ballast water is taken up when cargo is unloaded and released when cargo is loaded.

Buoyancy: Tendency of something to float in water.

Captive breeding: Breeding of rare animals in controlled 'captive' environments, such as zoos, reserves, laboratories, public aquaria, etc.

Ceramic: A substance made of clay (and sometimes metals) and permanently hardened by heat.

Citizen-scientist: A member of the public who collects information on the natural world as part of a collaborative project with scientists.

Colony: A group of animals (or plants) of the same species that live close together, usually for mutual benefit like protection or reproduction.

Conservation: The act of protecting, preserving or restoring something to prevent its loss or extinction.

Crustaceans: Animals of the class Crustacea, which have a hard shell, segmented body and jointed limbs – for example, shrimp, crabs and prawns.

CSIRO: Commonwealth Scientific and Industrial Research Organisation. Our national science research agency.

Deep-sea: The deeper, darker parts of the ocean beyond the continental shelf (200 metres); it's completely dark at 1000 metres or deeper.

EPBC Act: The *Environment Protection and Biodiversity Conservation Act* (1999) is Australia's national environmental law. It's used to legally protect threatened animals and plants.

Evolve/evolution: Develop gradually over a long period of time into a more complex life-form; undergo evolution.

Extinct/extinction: No known individuals of a species remain in the wild; the species is believed to have died out.

Fertilise: Provide the female's egg with male reproductive material (sperm) to cause it to develop into a baby animal – fertilisation.

Genetic diversity: The total number of genetic characteristics (genes) in the genetic makeup of an interbreeding population of a species. Greater diversity helps a population adapt to environmental change.

Habitat: The natural home or environment of an organism.

IUCN: International Union for Conservation of Nature. Its headquarters are in Switzerland and it publishes the Red List.

Juvenile: Young stages of an animal before it reaches sexual maturity or its adult form.

Larvae: The immature stages of an animal that transform into different forms as they become an adult.

Lure: Used to tempt an animal to do something – for example, fishing bait.

Marine: Existing in or produced by the sea.

Organism: A living thing – for example, a plant or an animal.

Plankton/planktonic: Tiny organisms drifting on currents near the surface of the sea; also includes the eggs and larvae of larger animals such as fish.

Population: A group of plants or animals that live in the same location and interbreed.

Public aquarium: A building that houses glass tanks filled with fish and aquatic organisms. Tasmania's Seahorse World and SEA LIFE Melbourne Aquarium are involved in handfish captive breeding.

Red List: Founded in 1964, it's the world's list of endangered animals and plants; each species is assessed against internationally agreed criteria on its risk of extinction.

Resilient: Able to withstand or recover quickly from difficult conditions.

SCUBA: Self-Contained Underwater Breathing Apparatus – a portable breathing device filled with compressed air; used by divers who stay underwater for long periods.

Sea Tulip: A sea-squirt (filter-feeding animal) that lives on rocks or the seafloor; it has a long stalk and the body is often covered by sponges.

Species: A group of organisms that have the same features and are capable of breeding and producing fertile offspring.

Specimen: An individual thing (for example, an animal) used as an example of its type (or species) for study or display.

Substrate: The underlying surface or material on which an organism lives.

Survey: To explore, examine, describe or measure something in order to find out more about it.

Swim bladder: A gas-filled sac in fish which helps control buoyancy; enables the fish to stay at a certain depth without floating up or sinking.

Volunteer: Someone who freely does work or a task without being paid.

Vulnerable: Exposed to the possibility of being harmed.

SPOTTED HANDFISH CONSERVATION TIMELINE

1960s / 1970s

Common handfish
In the 1960s and 1970s, Spotted Handfish were common. They were often seen by SCUBA divers and pulled up in scallop dredges.

Student learning
Some say Spotted Handfish were so common and easy to collect that the local university used them for dissections in zoology practical classes.

1980s

Invader arrives
In the early to mid-1980s, Northern Pacific Seastar juveniles arrived in the ballast tank water of Japanese tuna-fishing boats. When the ballast water was released in port, the seastars settled, grew and reproduced. Soon there were millions.

Vanished
In 1989, an Honours student at the University of Tasmania wanted to study the Spotted Handfish. But SCUBA divers couldn't find any. So they raised the alarm!

1990s

CSIRO scientific survey
Between 1990 and 1994, surveys of previously known Spotted Handfish sites found only 2 individuals.

Conservation status recognised
Listed as 'Threatened' under Tasmanian law in 1995, and as 'Endangered' in 1996 under Australian law. It's one of the first marine fish in the world to be listed as 'Critically Endangered' on the IUCN Red List.

Survey success
In mid-1996 CSIRO scientists found 3 small colonies of around 1000 Spotted Handfish in total.

Seastar plague
By 1995, the density of Northern Pacific Seastars in the Derwent Estuary was the highest of anywhere in the world, at 1000 per cubic metre.

Large-scale CSIRO scientific survey
In early 1996, a dedicated dive and trawl survey of 60 sites across the known distribution of Spotted Handfish found only 7 individuals.